REDEEM THE TIME

Stephen Kaung

ISBN: 978-1-942521-63-1

Available from:

Christian Testimony Ministry
4424 Huguenot Road
Richmond, Virginia 23235

www.christiantestimonyministry.com

Printed in USA

CONTENTS

CONFORMED TO THE IMAGE OF CHRIST

Ephesians 5:14-18—Wherefore he says, Wake up, thou that sleepest, and arise up from among the dead, and the Christ shall shine upon thee. See therefore how ye walk carefully, not as unwise but as wise, redeeming the time, because the days are evil. For this reason be not foolish, but understanding what is the will of the Lord. And be not drunk with wine, in which is debauchery; but be filled with the Spirit.

Let's pray:

Dear Lord, we want to thank Thee for gathering us together again before Thee. Lord, Thou hast been faithful. Thou hast been gracious to us that in these last days, in this difficult time, Thou hast gathered us to hear Thy word and to strengthen us that we may be Thy good army and be enabled to fight the good fight. Lord, we just commit ourselves to Thee. Speak, Thy servants are hearing. We ask in Thy name. Amen.

THE LORD JESUS CANNOT MARRY A CHILD

We thank God for giving us another opportunity to be together to hear God's Word and be better prepared for His imminent return. Every time God has given us such an opportunity, we really want to thank Him because it is His desire that we be prepared and made ready to be His bride. We know that any bridegroom is quite anxious to see the bride arrive, but our Lord Jesus, more than any bridegroom in the world, is anxious to come and claim His bride. However, He cannot come as long as the bride is not ready. I always remember what brother Lance Lambert said: "The Lord cannot marry a child. He has to have someone who is of His own stature that they may be united into one." So we thank God for the opportunities He has given us again and again to prepare for His return, and this is the reason why we are here.

THE LORD JESUS IS HEIR OF ALL THINGS

I think we all know that our theme is: "Redeem the Time". What is time? God lived before time, but He uses time to accomplish the tremendous purpose that is in His heart. The Bible tells us that even before the foundation of the world and before anything was created, God had in His heart a will—He wants His Son to be the heir of all things. He was thinking of creation and all of the things He would create in the heavens and on the earth. But God had a problem because He knows everything beforehand. He knew that the angels He created would rebel against Him, and He also knew the man that He would create later on would also rebel against Him. So how is He going to make all things come under the feet of His beloved Son? So may I use a human way of saying this: While He was considering this matter, His Son stepped in and said, "Father, go ahead; whatever Thou desires to do, I am willing to give Myself to be the Redeemer." And this is how God began to create all things. It all happened according to what God has foreknown.

ALL PROPHECIES BEFORE THE COMING OF THE LORD HAVE BEEN FULFILLED

Before the Lord Jesus left the earth He promised His disciples that He would go to prepare a place for them, and after He prepared that place, He would come back and receive them to Himself. This was a promise given over two thousand years ago; but century after century has passed and still He has not come. Nevertheless, that does not mean He will not come. We are now living in the beginning of the 21st century, and we can see how much closer we are to the coming of the Lord than anyone else before our century. Now there are some brothers and sisters who may be waiting for more prophesies to be fulfilled before the coming of the Lord, but let me tell you that all prophesies before the coming of the Lord have been fulfilled. That does not mean there are no more prophesies. There are still many prophesies concerning the coming of the Lord— during the coming of the Lord and after His coming. But notice that all prophesies preceding the coming of the Lord have been fulfilled, and the next event will be the coming of the Lord.

The Lord is coming. Hopefully, if by His grace we are prepared, then we can hasten His return. I will not say it depends on us because everything depends upon God, but I will say we are very important in this matter of His return. If by His grace we are prepared, ready, grown up, filled with the stature of Christ, He will not wait any longer; He will come back. So this is the burden in our hearts.

THE DAYS ARE EVIL

How can we redeem the time? We have already said that God uses time to accomplish His work. But God's enemy, the fallen angel, also knows there is a time and he is trying to postpone that time as much as possible. The only way he can do this is by enticing man not to be prepared and this will delay the return of the Lord. So this is the reason the world is getting worse and worse. Satan is trying every means to postpone the time. One of his ways to postpone the time is by trying to tempt God's people from being completed in Christ Jesus. That is why the Scriptures say, "The time is evil." We are living in days that are evil because God's enemy is trying very hard to prolong, to delay the coming of the Lord.

UNDERSTAND THE WILL OF GOD

So the exhortation from the Word of God is to walk carefully and do not be foolish so that we may understand the will of God. I am thinking especially of the young people. When we were young, I do not think we had all the temptations that they have today. We did have temptations but compared to today the young people are under greater temptations than ever before. The enemy tries to tempt the young people to love the world, but the Bible says, "Love not the world nor the things of the world," because the world is passing. The things of the world are passing; they are not permanent. We need to be aware of this and seek to do the will of God. Only by doing the will of God are we able to be better prepared for the return of the Lord.

EVERYTHING HAS BEEN PROVIDED
FOR THE MATURING OF THE SAINTS

The question is: How can we be better prepared? Who is going to prepare us? We thank God that He has made every provision for us. He has not only saved us, but the Bible says that He will save us to the uttermost. Therefore He has prepared everything for us to be matured, to be grown up and to be conformed to the image of Christ Jesus. But how? This is what I want to share with you dear brothers and sisters. In order to do that, we have to go back to the very beginning when we were saved.

We did not know when we were first saved that God had made provision for us to be grown up and matured in Christ Jesus. Of course, we know that before we were saved our spirit was dead. I often remember the Russian cosmonaut who went into outer space and came back and said, "There is no God because I looked around in space and did not see Him anywhere." Now isn't that foolishness! God is Spirit and the only way to contact God is by our spirit. You cannot contact Him with your mind or even with your body.

Many years ago I was in the Philippines, and in one of the cities I saw a church building so I went in. Near the pulpit I saw a few kneeling statues, but when I drew closer, I noticed they were nuns. They were kneeling before the altar motionless. My first reaction was how pious they were; but the Lord corrected me right away and said, "Worship is not an outward thing. You may appear to be very pious outwardly, but how about your heart?" So I learned a lesson that day.

Sins are Forgiven

Thank God He has made every provision for us to be matured. Of course, when He saved us, our sins were forgiven. I think for most Christians when they were first saved it was over the problem of their sins. That was what happened to me. How I thank God that He has washed away my sins! The sin burden fell from me, and I felt so light and free.

Our Spirit has been Cleansed, Renewed, Restored

However, that is the least of what the Lord has done for us because there are many positive things that God has done in saving us. Our spirit that was dead in sins and transgressions has now been cleansed, renewed and restored. There is a new spirit in each one of us, which is the reason we can now have fellowship with God. I remember praying as a child, but my prayer always hit the ceiling and came back. I never knew whether my prayer would be answered. But the day God saved me my connection with God was made. My spirit was brought to life, and by my spirit I could now contact God the Spirit. But more than that, the Lord Jesus came into my spirit to be life in my spirit. Now how good is that! Jesus Christ dwells in our heart to control our spirit, and by Him we are able to contact God.

The Holy Spirit Comes and Dwells in Our Spirit

More than that! Not only is Christ the life of our spirit, but the Holy Spirit of God also comes and dwells in our spirit. We have the Holy Spirit dwelling in us. Every brother and sister, everyone who is saved, not only has Christ as his life but also the Holy Spirit Who dwells in our spirit.

So the question is: Why does He dwell in our spirit? What is He working? What is His job? We know that the Holy Spirit who dwells in us has one job, one work, and that is to see that Christ grows in us. He can see what is not of Christ in us and will not only point it out but help us to get rid of it. That is why the Holy Spirit is in us.

So every brother and sister not only has Christ in him or her but also has the Holy Spirit dwelling within. He is very diligent. I believe from the very moment you are saved the Holy Spirit begins to work in your life. He is trying to bring you out of the world, out of yourself, and into Christ Jesus. I believe everyone probably has had that experience.

THE WORK OF THE HOLY SPIRIT INWARDLY

Sometimes we hear young people ask: "You talk about the Holy Spirit who dwells in us, but I do not feel Him. How do I know He is in me and is working?" I think that is very simple. After you are saved, I believe all of you will have this experience more or less. In the past you frequented undesirable places, but after you are saved, you may try to go there again, but a still small voice within you says, "You are now a Christian. Do you think it is a proper place for you to go?" Your response may have been, "Why not?" And you go. But after you went, you discovered that your communion with God was interrupted. And you cannot restore that communion with God until you confess your sin.

Probably this is a very common thing that will happen to you.

Or maybe before you were saved, you liked to boast, saying things that were not real which made you the center of your friends and made you feel very happy. But after you were saved, you tried boasting again and there was a still small voice telling you, "This is not true." I believe we all have had such an experience. When we continue to boast, are we happy about it? No. We find that we are miserable. And unless we confess before God and be true, our communion with God is interrupted. So in these small things, He will begin to deal with us.

THREE FUNCTIONS OF THE SPIRIT

Conscience

Our spirit has three main functions, one of them being the conscience. Often we hear people say, "I do everything according to my conscience." But our conscience was not dependable before we were saved because we did not have God's standard which had been lost when man sinned. After we were saved, that

11

standard was restored and now God is the standard of our conscience. In the world man's conscience follows the custom or the environment that he lives in; but we who are the Lord's live before God. Whenever we do something that does not bring peace to our conscience, our relationship with God is interrupted and our conscience will bother us. God has restored the proper use of our conscience, but until we cooperate with God our conscience will continue to accuse us. That is the way He is trying to purify us.

I will give an illustration of my experience. Even though I was a pastor's son I liked movies. Before I was saved, I used to spend my time on Saturday in the theatre. I had a friend who owned a theatre so I did not have to pay anything. When the newspapers came, the first page I looked at was the movie news. Now you may think a pastor's son probably would not do that; but I did. After I was saved, I still went to see movies, but my conscience began to bother me. I tried to argue, but it was no use; my conscience still bothered me. So I told the Lord, "If You do not like it, I will try not to go, but I will not tell anyone because I am not sure of myself. If I fail nobody will know." So for several months I did not go to the movies. My aunt told me, "You are a young man; have some fun. I will give you money to see a movie." But I could not. However, one day a religious movie came to Shanghai called "Noah's Ark", and someone sent us tickets. Now there was a struggle within me, and I said, "What is wrong with a religious movie?" So I went to that theater and looked at that movie for two hours; but what a fight went on inside of me! My conscience told me, "This is not the place you should be;" but I would not leave. I kept fighting and fighting inwardly the whole time. But thank God, that was the last time I went to a theater to see a movie. The Lord delivered me.

The Spirit of God is very real. He begins to work in us to purify and sanctify us that we may be totally God's and not of the world. The conscience of a person who is unsaved is not dependable because God is not the standard of his conscience. The custom of the world is his standard, and that is not dependable. After we are saved, God becomes the standard of our conscience. It is very important. The apostle Paul in witnessing before men and the Jewish council said, "I have lived my life with a good conscience." Another time he was with Felix the governor and he said, "I keep my conscience without offense before God and men." So to a Christian conscience is very important. We need to keep our conscience clear, and then we can stand before God and man.

Intuition

Now the Spirit of God not only works upon our conscience, He also works upon our intuition. We know that we usually learn from reading books or listening to lectures. We gather information from outside and store it in our mind as our data. That is the way we learn. But thank God, when He teaches us, He touches our intuition. It is not something from the outside that you absorb but it is within you. The Holy Spirit will speak to your intuition. Whatever He has done in your intuition that is the will of God. I John 2:27 says we have the unction, the anointing within us; that is to say, we have the Holy Spirit within us, and He will teach us in all things. Whatever He teaches is true. Whether it is big things or small things, He will teach us in all things. And if we follow His teaching, we will abide in Christ.

How do you know you abide in Christ? I remember once asking a group of young people this question, and they gave me different answers. Some said you need to read the Bible more, others said you need to pray more, and so forth. But the Bible says we have to listen to the teaching of the Anointing. The Holy Spirit within you is teaching you directly; therefore, intuitively you know what is right and what is wrong. When He is teaching you in this way and you obey, then you will discover you are growing in the Lord.

Worship

Not only that, our spirit has another function called worship. You remember in John 4 how our Lord Jesus talked to the Samaritan woman saying that we worship not in Jerusalem nor in Samaria but in spirit and truth. Deep in our spirit we worship God. That is the way the Holy Spirit is trying to grow us up in Christ Jesus.

THREE FUNCTIONS OF THE SOUL

But we not only have problems in our spirit, we have even more problems with our soul. When we are saved, Christ comes into our spirit to be the life of it, but we are still living in our soul. In other words, our soul's life is ourself. That is why in Romans 7 after Paul was saved, he discovered that it was as if he was two men. He knew God's will and wanted to do God's will, but there was another life in his soul which said 'no'. So he found that his "self" was stronger than his spirit. Oftentimes, he followed his "self" instead of Christ, and he longed for deliverance. So the Holy Spirit will not only touch our spirit but He will also deal with our soul.

Emotion

Within our soul is our emotion which is usually the clearest and most active part of our soul and needs the Holy Spirit to deal with it. You will remember in Matthew 10 that the Lord Jesus said, "If you love your father, mother, brother, sister, wife, and your own life more than Me, you are not worthy to be My disciples." What is wrong with loving our parents, our brothers and sisters, and even with loving our life? Isn't it in the Ten Commandments that we are to love our parents, honor our parents and we will have long life? What is wrong with that? This is not a matter of right or wrong but a matter of life. If we love the Lord more than anybody, more than our life, then we will love them even better in the right way. So our emotions need to be dealt with by the Holy Spirit. He will cleanse and allow us to have the right emotion. In other words, our emotion will not express ourselves but Christ.

Mind

Within our soul is our mind which is also very active, but the Lord will deal with it. You remember in Matthew 16 the Lord told Peter, "You are mindful of yourself instead of being mindful of God's will." So our minds need to be cleansed and redeemed.

Will

Also within the soul is our will. In Matthew 26 we find the Lord praying in the garden of Gethsemane: "Not my will, but Thy will be done."

COOPERATE WITH THE INDWELLING HOLY SPIRIT

So as we are talking about redeeming the time, in a practical way this is the way of redeeming the time. In other words, we need to cooperate with the indwelling Holy Spirit, and as we do that, not only our spirit but even our soul will be delivered. So that is the way to redeem our time.

Shall we pray:

Dear Lord, we want to thank Thee because Thou hast not only saved us, but Thou wants to save us to the uttermost. We praise and thank Thee that it is Thy will that we should be fully grown in Christ Jesus that we may be able to be His bride and glorify Him. Lord, we pray that Thy indwelling Spirit will work in us until Christ is fully formed in every one of us that we may be ready to meet Thee. This is our prayer. We ask in Thy name. Amen.

THE CALL TO OVERCOME

Revelation 1:1-3—Revelation of Jesus Christ, which God gave to him, to shew to his bondmen what must shortly take place; and he signified it, sending by his angel, to his bondman John, who testified the word of God, and the testimony of Jesus Christ, all things that he saw.

Blessed is he that reads, and they that hear the words of the prophecy, and keep the things written in it; for the time is near.

Revelation 2:7—He that has an ear, let him hear what the Spirit says to the assemblies. To him that overcomes, I will give to him to eat of the tree of life which is in the paradise of God.

("to him that overcomes" is repeated seven times in Revelation 2 and 3.)

Revelation 12:11—And 'they' have overcome him by reason of the blood of the Lamb, and by reason of the word of their testimony, and have not loved their life even unto death.

May we have a short word of prayer:

Lord, we do want to thank Thee for the privilege of being invited to Thy table. What can we say? Thou hast loved us to the uttermost, and Thou hast given Thyself totally to us. Lord, we thank Thee for the greatness of Thy redemption.

We thank Thee for the privilege of knowing Thee. We thank Thee for the privilege of being together again. We commit this time into Your hand and trust Thy Holy Spirit to do His work for the glory of God. In Thy precious name we pray. Amen.

The Book of Revelation is the revelation of Jesus Christ. Not only is the last book of the Bible the revelation of Jesus Christ, as a matter of fact, the whole Bible is the revelation of Jesus Christ. But there is a special blessing given in this book for those who read and for those who hear. I would like to share with you on this word that has been repeated seven times to each of the churches: "to him that overcomes."

EXILED FOR THE WORD OF GOD AND THE TESTIMONY OF JESUS

The apostle John was exiled to the island of Patmos for the Word of God and the testimony of Jesus. He was in his old age and the only remaining of the twelve original apostles. He was serving the Lord in the churches of Asia Minor, but in his old age he was exiled to the island of Patmos for the Word of God and the testimony of Jesus. He was sent to work in a mine on that island.

But on the Lord's day he was probably free. So I suppose he must have been sitting on a rock looking towards the coast of Asia Minor because on a good day you could see its outline. Probably he was thinking of the churches in Asia Minor in which he had served before he was exiled. While he was looking and maybe meditating, he heard a voice behind him like a trumpet, so he turned back to see that voice and saw what we call the Patmos vision. He saw seven golden lampstands and in their midst walked One like the Son of Man. This was the vision he saw on the island of Patmos.

Seven Golden Lampstands —Seven Churches

These seven golden lampstands that he saw are explained to us in the Bible. They represented the seven churches in Asia Minor at that time. Now of course we know there were more than seven churches in Asia Minor at that time. For instance, Colossae was not mentioned nor Hierapolis. But God purposely chose these seven churches in Asia Minor. We also know that these were actual churches in Asia Minor at that time, and this was there condition during the end of the first century. But Revelation, being a book of prophecy, I believe we can safely say these seven churches also represent the churches throughout the centuries. And we are now living in the beginning of the 21st century at the end of time. How much nearer must be the coming of the Lord!

THE LORD JESUS REVEALS A PORTION OF HIMSELF TO EACH CHURCH

The same calling goes out to each church, whether its condition is good or bad—the call to overcome. The Lord Jesus gives a revelation of Himself and then commits a portion of that revelation to each church. We know that our Lord Jesus is the fullness of the Godhead, and there is no way we can fathom how full He is. He is the fullness of grace, fullness of love, fullness of faith, fullness of everything. And to each of the churches He reveals a part of Himself as if to say that He is the fullness of the Godhead. There is no church on earth that can contain all His fullness. Each may be able to testify of part of the fullness of Christ, and when it is all put together, we begin to see the fullness of Christ. Whether the church has failed or whether the church is successful the last call is the same—the call to overcome.

THE LAST CALL OF GOD TO HIS CHURCH

So we believe this is the last call of God to His church—the call to overcome. If the seven churches in Asia in Revelation, chapters 2 and 3, stand for the churches of God towards the end of the first century, then century after century this same call remains. If we go through the book of Revelation, we will find this revealed. In chapters 2 and 3 there is the call to overcome, and it represents the call to God's churches during the end of the first century. In the latter part of chapter 7 we find there are countless number of people clothed in white and praising God. We think they represent the overcomers in the churches throughout the centuries. In chapter 12 there is the man child, and we believe that represents the overcomer towards the end of the age. Further on we find overcomers during the Great Tribulation because people are martyred for God during that time and they will sit on thrones. In chapter 19 there is the marriage of the Lamb and we believe it is the bride composed of the overcomers of the ages. Then in chapters 21 and 22 the new Jerusalem is the great consummation of all the works of God in the Old and New Testament time. Nothing is lost. This is what we find in the book of Revelation.

We believe that today, we who are living in the nearness of the coming of our blessed Lord, the same call has come to us—the call to overcome.

THE LAMB SLAIN FROM THE FOUNDATION OF THE WORLD

God has a supreme will, and that is the reason for creation. He loves His Son so much that He wants to give Him everything. He wants to make His Son heir of all things; in other words, everything will show a part of the glory of His Son. But we also know that because He is the One who knows the end from the beginning He knew there would be problems and trouble not only with the angels but even with man. That is why His Son offered Himself to be the Lamb. The Bible tells us that He was the Lamb slain from the foundation of the world. Even though our Lord Jesus as the Lamb was crucified on the cross in the beginning of the first century, yet in God's mind He is the Lamb slain *from* the foundation of the world. That is the love of God.

OVERCOMERS

Today, we are called to be overcomers. What is meant by overcomers? Overcomers are those who are able to respond to God's call. Whatever situation you may be put in God calls you to overcome—your surroundings, your circumstances, all the things that are happening in your life, the temptations that the enemy puts before you, the world. God wants you to overcome all these things for Christ and bring everything in your life to the feet of Jesus that He will have the preeminent place in your life and not yourself.

THE VISION OF THE MAN CHILD

We believe the call is urgent. We are living in a very important time. The Lord is coming, and it may happen any time. Suddenly, all over the world some people will disappear. They are the ones who have overcome and will welcome our Lord Jesus back to this world. In chapter 12 of the book of Revelation there is a great vision, and it is the time that we are now in.

A Woman of the Ages

In that great vision he saw a woman of the ages clothed with the sun. Who can the sun be except Christ? In other words, this woman is related to Christ. Then it says the moon is under her feet which represents the law; therefore she is related to the dispensation of the Law also. Upon her head there is a crown of twelve stars which represents the patriarch time of Abraham, Isaac, Jacob, and so forth. In other words, this is a woman of the ages. But at that time she represents the church on the verge of the coming of the Lord, and she is with child and travailing in birth. That is one great vision.

A Dragon

Then he saw another vision which was a dragon. I think we all know that the dragon represents Satan, the enemy, he and was before the woman. We know that the church has been and is Satan's enemy because she is being used by God to bring his end. The church is called by God to defeat God's enemy. We often say that for God to destroy Satan would be very easy. He could just say a word and it would be done, but that does not give glory to God. So God uses man who is a little lower than the angels to defeat Satan and his plan. So the dragon has been the enemy of the church ever since. Strangely, we find that even though the dragon was before the woman, he did not seem to care about her; he was waiting for the child to be born. Why is it so? Because the church, in a sense, has lost its testimony and is almost in the hands of the enemy. The church was not only unable to defeat the enemy, she was even defeated by the enemy so he did not seem to care about her in the last days. But he knew one thing—the child to be born would be his end so this is where his interest was focused. He waited before the woman to devour the child that was to be born. Now if he can do that he will postpone his days longer and even forever.

The Man Child is a Collective Term

Who is this child? People who study the Bible give us different interpretations, but I would like to share with you what I believe may be the most correct one. Some people say the child represents Christ. It cannot be because when this child is born, he is immediately raptured to heaven. But when our Lord Jesus was born, he was not immediately raptured to heaven but lived on earth thirty-three years. That is why we think it cannot be Christ. So if it is not Christ, who is that child? By reading chapter 12 we find that the child is a collective term. In other words, the child is not just one person; it represents people who have overcome as we find in chapter 12:11: "And they have overcome him by reason of the blood of the Lamb, by reason of their testimony, and have not loved their lives even onto death." So the child is a collective term and represents the overcomers living at the end days before the coming of the Lord.

THE MAN CHILD REPRESENTS THE OVERCOMERS LIVING AT THE COMING OF THE LORD

Again and again we have said that we are living in this very important time. The Lord is coming, and it depends on when the child is born. The last group of overcomers must be born before the coming of the Lord because as soon as the child is born, he is raptured to heaven. What happens after he is raptured to heaven? It is as if heaven is waiting for the child. In fact everything seems to be waiting for the child to be born and raptured. But once that happens the dragon is not able to touch the child. Now we all know from the Bible that the first heaven is the air surrounding us and is the headquarters of Satan and the fallen angels. But because this child has overcome he can go through the air and touch heaven. So we know this child represents the overcomers at our time.

The question is: Do you want to be among the rank? Are you ready for it? This child is able to go through Satan's headquarters, which is in the air, and reach heaven, and that means they have overcome. Sometimes people say, "As long as my two feet are within the door of heaven I am satisfied;" but will God be satisfied? He can only be satisfied if He can see us going through the air and reaching heaven to be the welcoming party for the coming of the Lord. Isn't that wonderful?

THE GREAT TRIBULATION

When the child is raptured to the throne, immediately there is war in the air. Michael and his angels will fight against Satan and his followers, and Satan will be thrown down from heaven upon the earth. In other words, the air will be cleared. We know that the first stage of the coming of the Lord will be from the throne to the air; that is why the air has to be cleared. Then the Lord with the overcomers of the last age will come from heaven to the air, and there will be great rejoicing in the heavens. What happens on earth? Satan is thrown down upon the earth and from the Bible we know the antichrist and the false prophet will also appear; therefore with the trio of evil on earth what can we expect but the Great Tribulation? This is where we find the three and a half years of the Great Tribulation.

The Christians who live in the last age but are not overcomers will have to pass through the Great Tribulation. The object of Satan's focus at that time will be the Christians who are still on earth and the Jews. It is the time of Jacob's trouble for the Jews, but God has already put His seal upon some of them and will keep them. However, the remaining Christians still have to go through the Great Tribulation. I believe you do not want to be among them. So far as God is concerned, He has given His people another chance, for out of the Great Tribulation there will be overcomers. There will be some who are faithful to the Lord who will be beheaded for the testimony of Jesus. These are the overcomers out of the Great Tribulation, and they will sit on the throne and reign with Christ. So you see the love of God. We may miss the chance, but He will give us another opportunity; He wants all of us to be overcomers.

AFTER THE GREAT TRIBULATION

After the Great Tribulation there will be the rapture of the remaining church—those who have died in Christ Jesus will be raised from the dead and those who are still living at that time. I Thessalonians 4 speaks of "those who are still living on the earth." This shows that there are those who are no longer living on earth because they have already been raptured alive. The overcomers and those who have been overcome will all be awakened and resurrected along with those who are still living on the earth after the Great Tribulation. They will be raptured together, not to the throne but to the air. This is the time when the whole church will be there together. During that period there will be no more Christians on earth, and the Bible tells us the seven vials, which is the wrath of God, will be upon this earth. During this time the judgment seat of Christ will be taking place in the air.

BELIEVERS WILL NOT BE
AT THE GREAT WHITE THRONE JUDGMENT

Thank God, we who believe in the Lord Jesus will not be judged at the great white throne judgment. One day God will set up His great white throne and will judge according to whatever unrepentant people have done upon this earth. That is a judicial judgment of eternal life or eternal death. But those whose names are in the book of life will not be judged at the throne judgment because Christ has been judged for us on Calvary's cross and has delivered us from the great judicial judgment; but that does not mean we as Christians will not be judged. We will be judged at the judgment seat of Christ.

THE JUDGMENT SEAT OF CHRIST

To understand the judgment seat of Christ I believe it would help to have some understanding of the custom of the east in the olden days with their large families unlike this country with its small families. I came from a large family with four generations living under one roof. It consisted of my grandfather and grandmother, their children, grandchildren, uncles and aunts, all living in one house, much like that found in the Bible. I lived in the midst of that big family, so I knew the blessing as well as the curse. My grandparents took care of everything. My grandfather paid for everything—our school, our weddings, all of our food. My grandmother took care of the food and practical things for the whole family. Therefore, people living in such a big house had nothing to do, and if you have nothing to do, what will happen? Gossiping and other worldly things. That is a big family, but God loves big families; He wants us to be with Him.

The judgment seat of Christ is not a judgment of life or death but one of reward or punishment. It is a family judgment, and only family members can attend that gathering. The head of the family will sit on a lifted place called a bema, and the whole family will gather to him in that room. He will tell who has brought glory to the family among his family members, and they will be praised and rewarded. But those who have brought disgrace upon the family will be punished, not with eternal death but with discipline. We do not like discipline, especially in our time; we want to be ourselves and free. But discipline is necessary for developing a good character. So those who have brought disgrace to the family of God will be disciplined during the time of the millennium or the thousand years, and those who are faithful to the Lord will rule and reign with Christ for a thousand years.

BE READY

Hopefully, we will be attracted by what the Lord has promised to us and be faithful to Him that we will be among the rank of the overcomers. I hope that when that day comes, every one of us here will disappear; none will be left. But if any should be left, woe to you. Thank God, you will have another chance because of the love of God.

Brothers and sisters, my last word to you in this conference is "be ready."

Shall we pray:

Dear Lord, we want to thank Thee for Thy boundless love towards us. How can we rebel against that love? Lord, we pray that every one of us here will yield to Thy great love and enable all that Thou hast prepared for us to be done in each and every one of us here. Lord, we want to glorify Thee as we have expressed ourselves during the

Lord's table. We pray that everyone here will give themselves to You and allow You to work out Thy full salvation in all of us. Lord, it is our blessed hope that we may see Thee face to face before the Great Tribulation shall come upon this earth. May Thy peace be with all the brothers and sisters. We ask in Thy precious name. Amen.

QUESTIONS AND ANSWERS

This is a question and answer time, but as usual I would like to say something before we have this time. The answer to all our spiritual problems is the Lord. We can only help a little and try to remove some hindrances; but I believe we all know that the One who solves our problems is the Lord Himself. So I hope you do not expect answers. You probably expect some help that will remove some of the hindrances, but we need to seek the Lord ourselves and get the right answer from Him.

REWARDS IN THE KINGDOM AGE

Q: Will the rewards that the overcomers receive from our Lord's judgment seat carry on into eternity or are these rewards only for the kingdom age of a thousand years?

A: I think probably the one who is asking this question hopes that the rewards to be had in the kingdom age will continue on to eternity. But unfortunately and fortunately, this is not the case. In other words, God's eternal purpose (Romans 8) is "whom He has called He has given grace." So God's purpose is that everyone who has been called and is faithful will be rewarded with the thousand-years' rule during the kingdom age. But if you are not faithful, you will miss the reward during that time.

There are some people who think that if everyone will eventually be in eternity as kings ruling with Christ, why bother? Maybe you are thinking about enjoying the two worlds—not only the spiritual but also the physical world. If you think you are wise in such a decision, then you are cheated because, how long can you live in this world? Maybe a hundred years? But even with a hundred years, how much can you enjoy the things of the world? However, the millennium is a thousand years. It is not that we are looking for rewards; what we really desire is to please the Lord and complete the eternal will of God.

So if we are faithful today, we will be rewarded during the millennial age. The Bible tells us we will rule and reign with Him; some will rule five cities, some will rule ten cities. However, we will all rule for God and not for ourselves, because if we are faithful today the Lord is able to entrust us with the rule in the thousand years.

We need to think of the eternal purpose of God when we will all be conformed to the image of God's Son. Once He has called us He will never leave us. He will continue to work in us until we are conformed to the image of Christ. If that process is delayed because of our carelessness in thinking we are going to enjoy the two worlds, the Lord knows better.

So think. All we can enjoy in this life is very limited—limited in time and in environment. How much can we really enjoy a world that is passing? The things of the world will all pass away; they are not eternal. So it is wise for us to be faithful to the Lord during the time we are still on this earth. But thank God, if we are faithful in this short period, the Lord will reward us with a thousand years of ruling with Him because He knows who is fit to rule. And this will be proven by the life that we are living in this age. So even though the reward will only be a thousand years, it is a tremendous reward.

Thank God, His eternal purpose is for everyone whom He has called to eventually be conformed to His image. What a promise! Every one of us who has been called, the end result will be that in eternity we will all be like Him and because of that we will all rule with Him as kings. So even though the thousand years reward is not for all, yet according to God's grace and purpose in eternity all who have been called will rule with Him as found in Revelation 22.

"And no curse shall be any more; and the throne of God and of the Lamb shall be in it; and his servants shall serve him, and they shall see his face; and his name *is* on their foreheads. And night shall not be any more, and no need of a lamp, and light of *the* sun; for *the* Lord God shall shine upon them, and they shall reign to the ages of ages" (vv.3-5). That is the wonderful promise of God.

WILL THE CHURCH FAIL IN THE END DAYS?

Q: In Revelation 12:4 the dragon ignores the woman and only waits for the child who is the overcomer. If the woman represents the church, does that mean the church will fail at the end time?

A: We know that according to the will of God His church is to be an overcoming church because He is the overcomer. So far as God is concerned, He does not expect the church to be overcome; His expectation is that she will overcome just as He has overcome. So what is it by which we overcome? I John 5 says, "This is the victory which has gotten the victory over the world, our faith" (v. 4b). In the heart of God He wants every one of us to overcome, and He has made every provision for us to overcome. So if we do not overcome or are being overcome, we cannot blame God. We are to blame because we do not appropriate the grace that He has already provided for us.

God has provided us with a new spirit, and Christ is the life of our new spirit. He also gives us the Holy Spirit to indwell us in order that the life of Christ will grow into maturity. So we find that God has given every provision for us to overcome. If we do not, it is because we do not appropriate what the Lord has provided for us.

However, that does not mean God has predestined the church to fail. It only means the church has failed to appropriate the grace, the mercy and the provision that God has provided for her. So we cannot say it is God's predestination that the church is to fail in the last days. That is not so. Even though God does foreknow everything, that does not mean He predestined it. We know from the Scriptures that He predestines the church to be an overcoming church, but if the church fails we cannot blame God; we have to blame ourselves. So the answer is: it is not God's predestination that the church will fail in the last days; it is only known by His foreknowledge, and we have to bear the responsibility.

OVERCOMING IN A FAILED CHURCH

Q: You exhorted us in your message to overcome in whatever circumstances we are in. Could you please elaborate on what an overcomer may look like in an assembly where it seems we are just going through the motions and routine? The desire to be submissive is still here, but there is a longing for the Lord to have so much more. Prayer is probably the key, but is there something more one can do?

A: What is the look of an overcomer? In Revelation 12:11 we are told who the overcomers are and what they do, which includes three things.

Number 1) "They overcome by the blood of the Lamb." This takes away any pride. We need the blood of the Lamb when we are unsaved to cleanse us from our sins. But as Christians we can never live beyond the need of the blood of the Lamb. The closer we are to the Lord the more we need the blood of the Lamb. We are told that even the tears of repentance need the blood of the Lamb. Throughout our whole life, we depend upon the blood of the Lamb which will take away any pride in us. Do not think you will ever outgrow the need for the blood of the Lamb. If you think that way, you are deceived. We are weak, and we need His blood forever.

And the closer we live to the Lord, the more we need the blood of the Lamb.

If you are placed in a certain situation such as Laodicea, what will you do? Because the church has failed, do you fail with it? No. You can open the door of your heart and invite the Lord in. He said that He would come in to you and eat with you. It means He will supply abundantly all your spiritual needs. Therefore, in spite of your environment in the church, if you open your heart to the Lord, He will come in and supply you abundantly with Himself, and you can be an overcomer in a failed church. You are not supposed to just go along with a church that has failed the Lord, but you are to be an overcomer in the midst of a failed church. It is by opening your heart to the Lord and letting Him come in that you will have a closer walk with the Lord. And of course you pray for the church you are in so that the Lord will guide and lead you, and if it is the Lord's will He may revive that fallen church.

If somehow you are put in such a situation, be faithful to the Lord; do not just follow the crowd. Open your heart to the Lord, have an intimate walk with Him and pray for the situation. I do not know what the Lord will do—whether He will change the situation in the church or whether He will lead you in another way. I do not know. The Lord has to make the decision. So we just commit where we are into the hands of the Lord and wait on Him.

That's all I can say. The Lord Himself is the only One who can guide and lead you. I know if you are in that situation it is difficult. But the Lord knows the answer, and the Lord is the answer and nobody else.

.

Other Books Printed By
Christian Testimony Ministry

SPEAKER	TITLE
DANA CONGDON	MARRIAGE, SINGLENESS, AND THE WILL OF GOD
	RECOVERY & RESTORATION
	THE HOLY SPIRIT
	HEBREWS
A.J. FLACK	TENT OF HIS SPLENDOUR
STEPHEN KAUNG	ACTS
	BE YE THEREFORE PERFECT
	CALLED OUT UNTO CHRIST
	CALLED TO THE FELLOWSHIP OF GOD'S SON
	DIVINE LIFE AND ORDER
	FOR ME TO LIVE IS CHRIST
	GLORIOUS LIBERTY OF THE CHILDREN OF GOD
	GOD'S PURPOSE FOR THE FAMILY
	I WILL BUILD MY CHURCH
	MEDITATIONS ON THE KINGDOM
	RECOVERY
	SPIRITUAL EXERCISE
	SPIRITUAL LIFE (II CORINTHIANS SERIES)
	TEACH US TO PRAY
	THE CROSS
	THE FULNESS OF CHRIST—IN THE BOOK OF REVELATION
	THE HEADSHIP OF CHRIST
	THE KINGDOM AND THE CHURCH
	THE KINGDOM OF GOD
	THE LAST CALL TO THE CHURCHES, THE CALL TO OVERCOME
	THE LIFE OF OUR LORD JESUS
	THE LIFE OF THE CHURCH, THE BODY OF CHRIST
	THE LORD'S TABLE
	TWO GUIDEPOSTS FOR INHERITING THE KINGDOM
	VISION OF CHRIST (REVELATION)
	WHO ARE WE?

WHY DO WE SO GATHER?
WORSHIP

LANCE LAMBERT

CALLED UNTO HIS ETERNAL GLORY
GOD'S ETERNAL PURPOSE
IN THE DAY OF THY POWER
JACOB I HAVE LOVED
LIVING FAITH
LESSONS FROM THE LIFE OF MOSES
LOVE DIVINE
MY HOUSE SHALL BE A HOUSE OF PRAYER
PREPARATION FOR THE COMING OF THE LORD
REIGNING WITH CHRIST
SPIRITUAL CHARACTER
THE GOSPEL OF THE KINGDOM
THE IMPORTANCE OF COVERING
THE LAST DAYS AND GOD'S PRIORITIES
THE PRIZE
THE SUPREMACY OF JESUS CHRIST
THINE IS THE POWER!
THOU ART MINE

T. AUSTIN-SPARKS

THE LORD'S TESTIMONY AND THE WORLD NEED

HARVEY CEDARS CONFERENCE

STEPHEN KAUNG

HEAVENLY VISION
SPIRITUAL RESPONSIBILITY

CONGDON, HILE, KAUNG

SPIRITUAL MINISTRY
SPIRITUAL AUTHORITY
SPIRITUAL HOUSE
SPIRITUAL SUBMISSION

STEPHEN KAUNG

SPIRITUAL KNOWLEDGE
SPIRITUAL POWER
SPIRITUAL REALITY
SPIRITUAL VALUE
SPIRITUAL BLESSING
SPIRITUAL DISCERNMENT

www.ingramcontent.com/pod-product-compliance
Lightning Source LLC
Chambersburg PA
CBHW060622030426
42337CB00018B/3151